Bedtime *and* Naptime...

and Bedtime and Naptime

Visit us at DeseretBook.com

Library of Congress Cataloging-in-Publication Data

Weeks, Hilary, author.

Bedtime and naptime . . . and bedtime and naptime : the simple joys of a mom's life / Hilary Weeks.

1 audio disc; 4¾ in.

Includes a compact disc containing music from Hilary Weeks.

Includes bibliographical references.

ISBN 978-1-60908-010-5 (hardbound)

1. Motherhood—Religious aspects—Church of Jesus Christ of Latter-day Saints. I. Title.

BX8641.W43 2011

248.8'431—dc22 2010045690

Printed in China

R. R. Donnelley, Shenzhen, China

10 9 8 7 6 5 4 3 2 1

Bedtime *and* Naptime...

and Bedtime and Naptime

The Simple Joys of a Mom's Life

HILARY WEEKS

DESERET BOOK

Salt Lake City, Utah

I have two hopes in writing this book.

The first one is that you will be reminded to laugh

. . . at the funny things that happen each day

. . . at yourself a little more

. . . in the moment, instead of waiting for it to be "funny someday"

. . . when you might otherwise cry

And, if for no other reason,

. . . to strengthen your abdominal muscles.

The second hope is that you will feel

. . . the power of your influence as a mother

. . . the love and support of our Heavenly Father

. . . that you can do all you have been asked to do

. . . inspired to continue giving your best

. . . a desire to fill another sippy cup, make another meal, find another missing shoe, and wipe another food-covered, chubby-cheeked face.

It all started when I changed the lyrics to the song "My Favorite Things" from *The Sound of Music.*

Sure, I like raindrops on roses and whiskers on kittens, bright copper kettles and warm woolen mittens. Who doesn't? (Except that wool does make me itch.)

But that song didn't really capture my *favorite things.*

My "favorites" would look more like this:

When I don't constantly **nag** at my children—
They just do their chores, like sweeping the kitchen.
When they put toilet paper back on the roll,
It feels like I've witnessed a *small miracle.*

Bedtime and naptime and bedtime and naptime
Bedtime and naptime and **bedtime and naptime.**
Did I mention it's nice when the kids go to sleep?
These are a few of my favorite things.

It was so much fun to change the lyrics and sing about a day in the life of a mother that I just kept on changing lyrics (*and diapers*)!

There are no more diapers to be changed at our house, but the *joys of being a mom* still continue. This book and CD are filled with a few of my favorite . . .

Quotes

Experiences

Memories

Insights

Recipes

And moments of motherhood.

Perhaps it will remind you of a few of *your favorite things*, too.

One day when I was doing the dishes, my daughter said to me,

"Mom, are you mad?"

I replied, "No."

She followed with a second, more probing question.

"Then why does your face look like that?"

So, in the words of a beloved Primary song, I offer this reminder (*mostly for myself!*)

No one likes a frowning face.
Change it for a *smile*.
Make the world a better place
By *smiling* all the while.

Recently, after purchasing some new school clothes, my sixteen-year-old daughter reorganized her closet.

All the shirts were in one section.

All the pants were in another.

The shirts were organized according to the color wheel, and the hangers all hung the same direction.

I didn't offer her closet organizing tips. I've never said anything about how to arrange clothes. I didn't give a single suggestion. And she didn't ask.

But later, when I looked in her closet, I realized it was organized . . .

Exactly like mine.

One afternoon, I was making some orange rolls *for dinner*. When I was almost done, I received the prompting that if I wanted a rotisserie chicken (which I would need for the soup I was also going to make), I needed to go to the store right after making the rolls. I was about to leave when I remembered an e-mail I wanted to send. **What difference would thirty seconds make?** I sent the e-mail and headed for the store.

Upon arriving at the store, I went directly to the rotisserie chicken stand. I walked up just in time to see a lady stop in front of the stand, eye the very last chicken, and then pick it up and put it in her cart! **I couldn't believe it!**

I wanted to say to her, "That's *my* chicken! Did you have any impressions or feelings about that chicken? Because I did!"

If only I hadn't sent the e-mail.

Turns out **thirty seconds** *did* **make a difference.**

I went to the deli counter and asked if they had any more chickens. The employee said, "No. For some reason the chickens have been selling really fast tonight."

I was able to find another option, and dinner went on. But as I thought about what had happened, I was so grateful I had seen the last chicken snatched up. If I had walked up and seen the whole stand empty, I would have thought it wouldn't have mattered how fast I got there. Instead, I was reminded that I need to follow the promptings I receive with exactness.

Thank goodness Heavenly Father reminded me of that principle using a rotisserie chicken, helping me to get it right now so I'd do better in the future when it really mattered.

I was reminded of something else as well. Heavenly Father cares about every detail of our lives. He cares about rotisserie chickens!

He cares about the big stuff, the medium stuff, and the very tiniest things in our lives.

And He will be as much a part of our lives as we will let Him be.

What your children really want for dinner is *you*.

DALLIN H. OAKS

A new tradition can start anytime.

One of our family favorites started just three years ago, a few weeks before Thanksgiving.

I bought a big piece of white butcher paper and taped it to a wall in the kitchen area. At the top I wrote, "Things We Are Grateful For . . ." and I placed colored markers nearby. Each time we thought of something we were thankful for, we wrote it on the poster. Even friends who visited our home were invited to write something.

Our gratitude poster was filled with words—big, small, cursive, printed, bubble-lettered, misspelled, and, most of all . . .

heartfelt.

One year, our four-year-old wrote her name on the poster at least fifteen times.

(I still giggle when I think about that.)

He is a *wise man* who docs not grieve for the things which he has not, but *rejoices* for those which he has.

EPICTETUS

Cheese Dish

(I know, it's a lackluster title, but that's what we call it. And believe me and my taste buds when we tell you, this breakfast dish is delicious!)

The recipe comes from the kitchen of my mother-in-law, Jo Weeks. I would have married Tim just to get this recipe. We always devour it on Christmas morning and general conference weekend.

4 eggs, separated
1 pound shredded Monterey Jack cheese
1 pound shredded cheddar cheese
1 can (12 ounces) evaporated milk
1 can (4 ounces) diced green chilies
1 Tablespoon flour
½ teaspoon salt
½ teaspoon pepper

Beat egg whites until stiff. Spread cheeses in bottom of a greased 9 x 13 baking dish. In a separate bowl, combine evaporated milk, chilies, egg yolks, flour, salt, and pepper, then gently fold into egg whites. Pour mixture on top of cheese. Bake for one hour at 325° F.

Now, this is kind of a personal question:

Do you have a problem or an "issue" with tags in your clothing? **Do they itch?** Do you have to cut them out? I do!

Recently I cut a tag out of a shirt. I read the tag so I would know how to launder the shirt properly. I was a bit *surprised* by the directions—I've never seen this before:

I don't consider myself a laundry expert. I throw clean clothes on the floor—I rarely fold them right as they come out of the dryer. But for heaven's sake, I certainly know not to bake my shirt in a machine.

Did they think I was going to put it in a casserole?

Then, not long after that, I
cut another tag out of a shirt.
Again—*very curious*
instructions.

It is the third line
that gets me:

Away from what? They didn't finish the sentence! What am I not supposed to dry it next to? Oh, come on, don't leave me hanging like this! Am I not supposed to dry it next to

. . . string cheese?

. . . the TV?

. . . the dog?

. . . strangers?

That must be it:

Dry flat away from strangers!

Since the discovery of those two very unusual tags, I've become an *avid tag reader*. I read my tags, Tim's tags, the kids' tags—I'll even stop and read tags at the store.

Imagine my *surprise* when I came across this tag . . .

Rejoice,
again I say,
Rejoice!

Occasionally I post *quotes and scriptures* on my bathroom mirror and memorize them in the morning while poofing and spraying my hair. I wish I could say I can still quote each one, but I've forgotten here and there. In fact, I attended a class on *improving memory*. When I told my friend I was going, she said . . .

"Forget about it. You've had four children; your memory isn't coming back."

The first quote I chose to memorize is one of my all-time favorites. I can tell how difficult a quote is to **memorize** by how much hairspray I go through while I'm learning it.

This one took a *full bottle.*

[The Spirit] quickens all the intellectual faculties, increases, enlarges, *expands*, and purifies all the natural passions and affections; and adapts them, by the *gift of wisdom*, to their lawful use. It inspires, develops, cultivates, and matures all the fine-toned sympathies, joys, tastes, kindred feelings, and affections of our nature. It inspires *virtue*, kindness, goodness, tenderness, gentleness, and charity. It develops *beauty of person*, form, and features. It tends to health, vigor, animation, and social feeling. It invigorates all the faculties of the physical and intellectual man. It *strengthens* and gives tone to the nerves. In short, it is, as it were, marrow to the bone, joy to the heart, light to the eyes, music to the ears, and *life to the whole being*.

PARLEY P. PRATT

What seems to be the question that moms are asked more than any other?

You got it . . . "What's for dinner?"

Sometimes I would like someone else to answer that question.

Yeah, what *is* for dinner? And who wants to make it?

Well, this recipe has *your* back. This recipe is on *your* side.

It has only four ingredients and is a **cinch** to make.

Is it delicious, you ask?

Umm . . . it will pretty much make your family involuntarily volunteer to do the dishes.

Now, that's what I'm talking about.

Bacon-Wrapped Chicken

3 large chicken breasts, sliced in half down the middle
  to make 6 pieces
6 Tablespoons chive-and-onion cream cheese
6 Tablespoons margarine
6 pieces of bacon, uncooked

Pound the six chicken halves to tenderize and flatten, being careful not to tear. On top of each flattened chicken breast, place a tablespoon of cream cheese and a tablespoon of margarine. Roll up each breast and wrap with a piece of bacon. Place bacon-wrapped chicken in baking dish. Cover and cook for 30 minutes at 375 degrees Fahrenheit. When juices run clear and chicken is cooked through, uncover dish and turn oven to broil. Broil until bacon reaches desired crispness.

When serving, be sure to pour the *yummy* juices from the baking dish over the chicken. You might be tempted to sip it with a straw . . . but don't, that's *embarrassing*.

Once in a while, before I retire to bed, I quietly slip into my daughters' rooms, where they are fast asleep.

I tuck their hair behind their ears, lean over, and softly whisper . . .

I believe in you.

I made a cake. I know, big accomplishment.

On the back of a cake mix box, I found a recipe for a sort of jazzed-up yellow cake with brown-sugar-crumbly things in the middle. It looked good, so I tried it. I was talking on the phone while I read the new recipe and mixed the ingredients together.

After baking the cake for about fifteen minutes, I realized I had **left out the butter!** The recipe called for a whole cube of it! Ugh! I was frustrated with myself for getting distracted by the phone and ruining the cake. Not to mention all the time and supplies I had wasted.

Out of curiosity, I let the cake finish baking. When the timer went off, the cake looked normal. It smelled normal. Lo and behold—it *tasted* normal! **It was actually really good!** I was quite pleased with the fact that I had cut out all of that unnecessary fat. (I know, it was by accident, but I was still happy with myself.)

Once in a while I pause to see if there is any "unnecessary butter" being added to my day. Sometimes I find things that I can cut out without even missing them. They were just filling up my day and weighing me down.

The *important ingredients for success* are the ones I make sure I add to my day.

Paper plates.

Now that's *my* kind of invention.

It may seem simple
All the little things you do
But the *lives you touch* matter so much
And there's no one else like you
And Father needs you to be strong and faithful
To be all you can be
Oh, if you could see what *He sees*
You'd believe in what you're doing
You'd believe in who you are
Hold tight to the truth that
you're a daughter of God
Believe in who you're becoming
Believe in who you are

Without being too presumptuous, may I suggest something you might not have considered until now . . .

We all name our pets—our dogs, cats, fish, and so on. Some of us even name our cars. We name the things we love, the things that are important to us. So, let me ask you this, *is your washing machine important to you?* (Yes.) Do you love it? (Of course.) Could you live without it? (Never!)

Well then, have you named your washing machine?

Think of all it does for you! What have you done for your washing machine lately?

Now, you don't have to go crazy, but I would suggest spending some quality time together. Involve your washing machine in some family activities. Sure, it's a little awkward and heavy to take with you, but I know from my own experience with my washing machine, *Wynona,* that those moments mean so much. We've become so close.

Here are a few things I have done to strengthen the relationship I have with my washer. You don't have to do these same things, just be creative—find ways to connect with *your washer.*

Include your washer in family photographs.

Take your washing machine on vacation.

WE did!

You have to do laundry anyway, right?

Washing machines love water of all kinds—
hot, warm, cold, hot-cold, warm-warm . . .
so *take your washer to the beach!*

World's Best Cheeseball

This is, hands down, the *best recipe* I own. My Aunt Gayle made this for all our family holiday gatherings, and now I make it for all of mine. After tasting it, people think I'm a hero. Trust me—make this for your next special occasion and you will be a hero too. Don't be surprised if someone breaks out singing, *"Did you ever know that you're my hero?"* It's that good.

1 package (8 ounces) cream cheese
1 jar (5 ounces) Kraft Old English Cheese Spread
4 Tablespoons crumbled blue cheese
2 or 3 green onions, diced
2 teaspoons Worcestershire sauce
Chopped pecans

In mixer, thoroughly combine cheeses, green onions, and Worcestershire sauce. Form into ball and roll in chopped pecans. Place on a pretty plate. Serve with favorite snack crackers.

Don't worry about
what other people
think of you;
worry about what
they think of
themselves when
they're with *you*.

If I only had today
I'd hold you and listen
I'd memorize every detail of *your face*
I'd tell you I loved you over and over
I wouldn't let excuses get in the way
Then I'd remind you of *forever*
And how our love would never change
If I only had today

A few thoughts on mothering from Elder M. Russell Ballard:

First, recognize that the joy of motherhood comes in *moments.* There will be hard times and frustrating times. But amid the challenges, there are *shining moments* of joy and satisfaction. . . .

Second, don't overschedule yourselves or your children. . . . Families need unstructured time when relationships can deepen and real parenting can take place. **Take time to listen, to laugh, and to** ***play together***.

Third, even as you try to cut out the extra commitments, sisters, find some *time for yourself* to cultivate your gifts and interests. Pick one or two things that you would like to learn or do that will enrich your life, and make time for them. Water cannot be drawn from an empty well, and if you are not setting aside *a little time* for what replenishes you, you will have less and less to give to others, even to your children.

Pray each day to
see *miracles*. . .
and you will.

As a young mother with a gaggle of girls, I quickly realized that gone were the days of having big chunks of uninterrupted time to focus on and complete projects.

Initially, I was frustrated with having only fifteen minutes here and twenty there to work on things that were important to me.

But then I discovered something wonderful . . .

Heavenly Father can help us **do amazing things** during brief but productive and consistent amounts of time. He can **magnify** our efforts and **multiply** our output.

I have written more than a hundred songs using fifteen minutes here, twenty minutes there.

Small *moments* can become significant *accomplishments.*

There are lots of

right ways

to do everything.

VIRGINIA H. PEARCE

When the kids fight

When my husband's late

When I'm feeling sad

I open the freezer, pull out the *ice cream*,

and then I don't feel so bad!

I keep a black, moleskin notebook in my scripture case. In it I record inspiration and insights I receive while studying the scriptures, listening to talks, and so on. But there is something else I record in this notebook:

"Days to Remember"

Once in a while there are days that are so close to perfect, I never want to forget them. I want to read about them again and again and enjoy the flood of memories for the rest of my life.

When my life is in the sunset years and my days are quiet and contemplative, I won't have to worry or wonder if I made meaningful memories. Those experiences will be right there on the pages—recorded and remembered.

There never was
a child so lovely,
but his mother was
glad to get him
asleep.

RALPH WALDO EMERSON

I have discovered that very often the Spirit speaks to me in the *midst of everyday activities* like doing the dishes, making beds, and folding laundry.

I opened the linen closet to put away towels, and received inspiration. If you could see my linen closet, you might assume that what I was being inspired to do was to clean it. However, the inspiration was a bit more profound.

The Spirit brought to my mind the thought that Heavenly Father spends a great deal of time and effort trying to *convince* His children that *He loves them*. Some of them feel His love openly and easily. Some are harder to convince.

He whispers His love through answered prayers, calming thoughts, peace, and tender mercies. *Endless are His evidences of love.*

Then the Spirit expounded . . .

As a mother, I can help. I can play an important part in helping Him achieve this vital, soul-saving objective.

If my children feel and *know* of my love for them, it will make it easier for them to accept, feel, and know of Heavenly Father's love for them.

Every kiss,
hug,
kind word,
prayer,
sacrifice,
example,
high-five
will make a difference.

I am convinced that *a mother's love is a gateway* through which children can feel Heavenly Father's love.

Yummiest Punch You Could Ever Serve at a Party

(and the easiest too!)

In a large punch bowl, mix together

1 can white grape raspberry concentrate (undiluted)
1 bottle (2 liters) pineapple soda
1 bag of crushed ice

Could it really be *that* simple?

Yep.

Are people going to *love* it?

Double yep.

Several years ago, on **Labor Day Eve,** Tim and I realized we had **no plans** for the following day.

A day off from school and work
and we had *no plans?*

That just didn't seem right. So we brainstormed all the usual options—a movie, perhaps a movie, we could go see a movie, maybe a movie would be good.

Uninspired, we **dug a little deeper**, got a little more creative.

The next morning we pulled four miniature Christmas trees from storage and decorated them.

Then we listened to *Christmas music* as we drove to a Mexican restaurant for lunch. (We always eat Mexican food on Christmas Eve.)

After lunch, we divided into "teams" and shopped—each person would receive two gifts purchased at the dollar store.

We wrapped the gifts, put them under the trees, and gathered later that night to open them. (I would be too embarrassed to tell you that one daughter received a very large pair of pink polyester underwear.)

Never mind that it wasn't really Christmas.

That day became a gift.

I can't remember the specifics of a single other Labor Day; my family probably can't either. But ask any of them and they could tell you the details of this one.

That day was . . .

Unique, Fun, *Memorable*.

Extraordinary moments can happen in the middle of ordinary days.

I was on a mother-daughter dinner date with Calli, who was nine at the time. Through a mouthful of macaroni and cheese, Calli giggled as she recounted a game of freeze tag she played during recess that day.

Then it hit me . . .

I will spend eternity knowing Calli as an adult. But tonight, right here, right now, and for the next few precious years, I have the rare privilege of knowing her *as a child.*

What a gift to experience the children in our lives as children!

For a brief moment during the journey of mortality, we get to watch them laugh, learn, experience, grow.

Yes, in the middle of an ordinary day,
it was an extraordinary moment.

I had just delivered baby number four.

I was a sleep-deprived, hormone-filled, drained, depleted mother. What I needed was a day at the spa, a vacation, a massage, or at the very minimum to sleep in just one morning.

One.

But instead, "people" wanted lunches made before leaving for school. They wanted me to read to them, help with homework, tie their shoes, cut their sandwiches in half, wash their clothes, find their shin guards, take them to piano lessons, and pour them ketchup.

I wanted to go on strike, threatening to never again microwave another chicken nugget. Instead, I went to the adult session of stake conference.

Heavenly Father sent a message to me—right at the beginning, during the opening hymn, "How Firm a Foundation." These words comforted my weary soul:

As thy days may demand,
so thy succor shall be.

Oh, how I needed that message.

I was still tired. But that promise gave me the courage to keep going, knowing that the Savior would be by my side each day to offer the support and strength I needed.

And He kept His word.

When mothers know
who they are and
who God is and have
made covenants with
Him, they will have
great power and
influence for good
on their children.

JULIE B. BECK

When it's hard to believe in yourself

When you feel like you're beginning to doubt

Remember . . .

That He believes in what you're doing

He believes in who you are

Don't lose sight of the truth that you're a

daughter of God

And He believes in who you're becoming

He believes in

Who you are

Sources Cited

Page 7. "No one likes a frowning face . . ." "Smiles," *Children's Songbook* (Salt Lake City: The Church of Jesus Christ of Latter-day Saints, 1989), 267.
Page 13. Dallin H. Oaks, "Good, Better, Best," *Ensign*, November 2007, 106.
Page 24. "Rejoice, the Lord Is King!" *Hymns of The Church of Jesus Christ of Latter-day Saints* (Salt Lake City: The Church of Jesus Christ of Latter-day Saints, 1985), no. 66.
Page 27. Parley P. Pratt, *Key to the Science of Theology* (London: Latter-day Saints' Book Depot, 1855), 98-99.
Page 49. M. Russell Ballard, "Daughters of God," *Ensign*, May 2008, 109-10.
Page 71. "As thy days may demand . . ." "How Firm a Foundation," *Hymns*, no. 85.
Page 72. Julie B. Beck, "Mothers Who Know," *Ensign*, November 2007, 76.

Photo Credits

Page 1: © Brooke Fuller/Shutterstock Images
Pages 2, 37, 66: © Hemera/Thinkstock
Page 4: © design56/Shutterstock Images
Page 6: © Digital Vision/Getty Images
Page 9: © Jupiterimages/Comstock Images/Getty Images
Page 10: © R. Ashrafov/Shutterstock Images
Pages 12, 47, 71, 74: © iStockphoto/Thinkstock
Page 22: © viviamo/Shutterstock Images
Page 25: © Brand X Pictures/Jupiterimages
Page 28: © Jacek Chabraszewski/Shutterstock Images
Page 31: © David De Lossy/Valueline/Thinkstock
Page 33: © Martin Poole/Photodisc/Thinkstock
Page 34: © Kevin Dyer/iStockphoto
Page 39: Photo by Kathryn Turley
Page 44: © Jupiterimages/BananaStock/Getty Images
Page 48: © Slobodan Zivkovic/Shutterstock Images
Page 51: © albinutza/Shutterstock Images
Page 52: © Kzenon/Shutterstock Images
Page 54: © Martin Poole/Digital Vision/Thinkstock
Page 57: © Darryl Brooks/Shutterstock Images
Page 58: © Eduard Stelmakh/Shutterstock Images
Page 61: © Gladskikh Tatiana/Shutterstock Images
Page 63: © angelakatharina/Shutterstock Images
Page 68: © David Woolley/Digital Vision/Thinkstock
Page 73: © Felix Mizioznikov/Shutterstock Images
All other photos appear courtesy of the author.